SHARKS!

PHONICS

Great Big Sharks

Book 8: r-blends

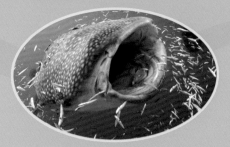

By Quinlan B. Lee

Photo Credits: cover: Mauricio Handler/National Geographic; title page: Reinhard Dirscherl/age fotostock Spain S.L./Corbis; pages 2-3: Robert Essel/Corbis; pages 4-5: A̶̶̶̶̶̶̶ ̶ ̶ ̶ ̶ ̶tock; page 6: Jurgen Freund/Nature Picture Library/Corbis; pages 8-9: Fred Bavendam/Minden Pictures/Corbis; ̶̶̶totstock Spain S.L./Corbis; page 12: Mauricio Handler/ National Geographic; pages 14-15: ̶ ̶ ̶ ̶ ̶ ̶ ̶ ̶ ̶ ̶ ̶ ̶ ̶ ̶ ̶ ̶ ̶ ̶ ̶ Mauricio Handler/National Geographic.

ISBN 978-0-545-74707-3

12 11 10 9 8 7 6 5 4 3 2 1   14 15 16 17 18/0

Printed in China   145

First Printing, September 2014

SCHOLASTIC INC.

Try to guess what this shark is called.

It **grows** as big as a **truck**.

This **great** big shark is called a whale shark.

Even though they have "whale" in their name, they are not whales.

They **breathe** through gills, so they are fish.

Whale sharks are the biggest fish.
They are also the biggest sharks.

Whale sharks are **gray**. They have white or yellow spots on their **broad** backs. These spots are like fingerprints. Each whale shark's spots are special.

Whale sharks are **great** big sharks.
But their **prey** is very small.

They only eat small fish, small **crabs**, and small shrimp called **krill**.

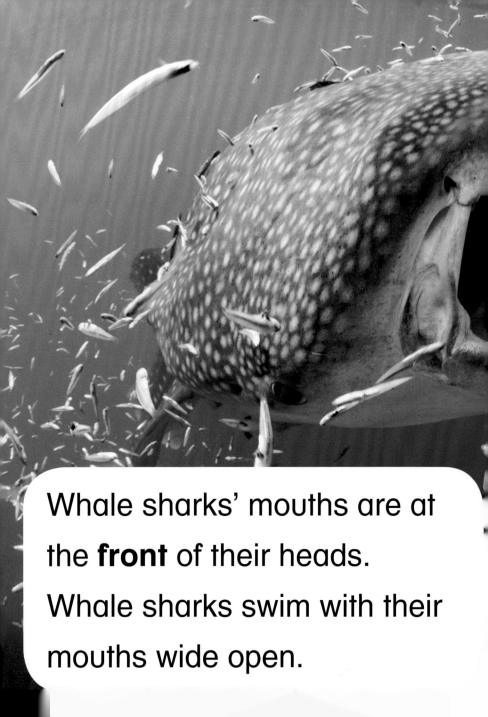

Whale sharks' mouths are at the **front** of their heads. Whale sharks swim with their mouths wide open.

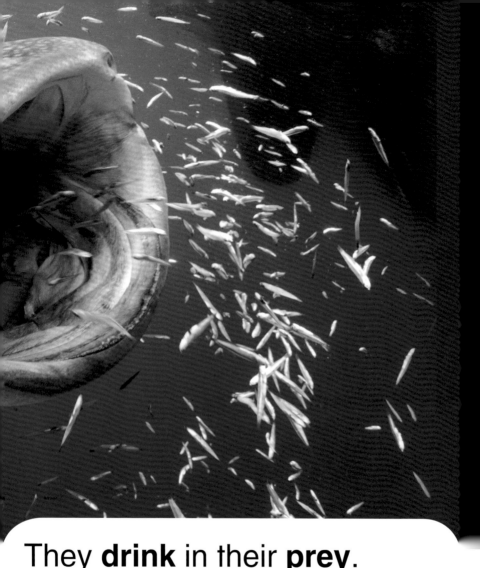

They **drink** in their **prey**.
Then they close their mouths
and **trap** the **prey** inside.

Whale sharks are **great** big sharks, but they are shy. Whale sharks do not swim in a **group**. You will only find a **crowd** if there is a lot of **krill**.

These **great** big sharks can be our **friends**.
They only hurt people if they **crash** into them with their fins.

Some people even like to swim with them.

They **grab** their fins and go for a ride.

Would you like to **try** that?